To:

From:

to Imogen Beatrice and Helena Blythe

Library of Congress Cataloging-in-Publication Data

Hegg, Tom.
Baby talk : reflections on a blessed event / written by Tom Hegg.
pages cm
ISBN 978-0-931674-45-7 (alk. paper)
1. Parent and child. 2. Infants. 3. Childbirth. I. Title.
HQ755.85.H438 2013
306.874--dc23   2013003513

Text copyright © 2013, Tom Hegg
Illustrations copyright © 2013, TRISTAN Publishing, Inc.
All Rights Reserved
Printed in China
First Printing

TRISTAN Publishing, Inc.
2355 Louisiana Avenue North
Golden Valley, MN 55427

To learn about all of our books with a message please visit
www.TRISTANpublishing.com

Baby Talk

Reflections on a Blessed Event

by Tom Hegg

TRISTAN PUBLISHING
Minneapolis

A note from the Author

Thank goodness for all those "How-To" baby books! So many of them were of such help in the days when we were raising our own little family. Now, in what seems like no time at all, our granddaughters have come into the world. Believe me, we continue to need all the wisdom we can glean from any and all sources.

But this book focuses on the "Why-To" rather than the "How-To". There are so many surprises in store... so many blessings and bumps along the way that you never see coming... no matter how careful and thorough have been the preparations of body, mind and spirit for the arrival of a new life.

"Baby Talk - reflections on a Blessed Event" is meant for anyone - Mom and Dad, Grandma and Grandpa, Brother and Sister, Aunt and Uncle... all who find themselves within the circle of love that only the arrival of a baby can create. Let's talk.

TH

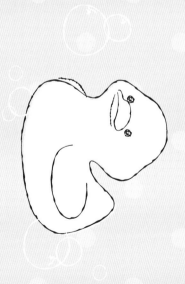

We thought we were beyond prepared... We'd taken every class,
Digested all the how-to books, and filled the car with gas.

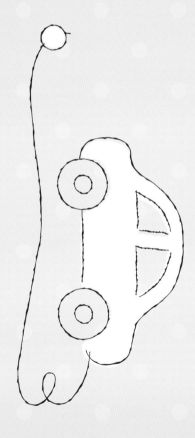

Our home was baby-proofed from stem to stern, and clever toys
Adorned a nursery designed for either girls or boys.

And then, The Big Day came! Our planning stood us in good stead.
It all went just like clockwork, and I kept a level head.

But hold your horses…. Here's the deal: No book on any shelf

Prepares you for the way you feel. You find out for yourself.

The doctor said, "You have a son. Ten fingers and ten toes."

An overture began... the lights went up... the curtain rose...

We inked a lifetime contract at the moment of his birth…
Just think… The Parents of The Greatest Little Show on Earth!

It hit me... I had never, ever felt this way before...
As if some inner switch had tripped, I changed forevermore.

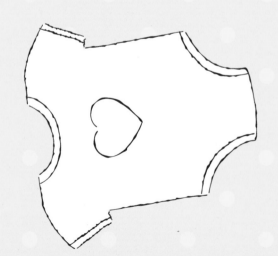

That little bundle had my chin! He also had my heart,
And, (should he ever need it from me), any other part.

I knew, without a moment's hesitation or regret,
I'd gladly give my life for him… and still be in his debt.

No more was I to wring my hands and moan, "What means it all?"
Who's got the time? You have to change their drawers and watch them crawl.

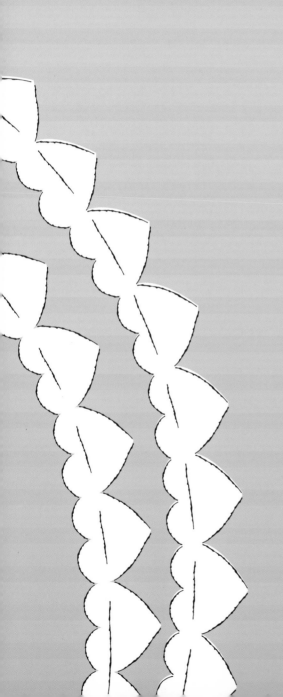

For us, there is no question; not the shadow of a doubt....
You love them more than life itself, and that's what life's about.

You also die a death whenever they get hurt or sick,
And come to know your knees when medicine won't do the trick.

The coverage of children being victimized by war,
Or any other horror here, or any foreign shore,

Will haunt you, and demand of you: Suit up, and take a stand,
And give as much as you can give, and lend a helping hand.

You get them into daycare, and you fret that they're ignored.
You try so hard to keep your cool, but go and blow your gourd.

Apology accepted. Leaving teeny beans is tough.
They know you didn't mean it. Nothing's ever good enough.

Titanic tantrums rupture that embarrass you to bits,
And try your patience, sanity, maturity and wits.

Oh, look! We have an audience! The more of them around,
The bigger is the drama, and the louder is the sound.

By night, they scream like banshees, and refuse to go to sleep.
You walk the floor with them until your arms ache, and you weep.

They finally conk out. You lay them gently in the crib....
And as you watch them slumber... think about another sib.

First tooth. First solid food. First word. First step. First locks get shorn. First overnight. First summer camp. First kiss. First love. First born.

Like ice cream cones and fireworks, it all goes pretty fast.
You look away, and suddenly, the future is the past.

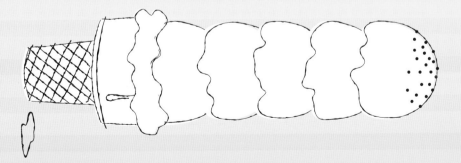

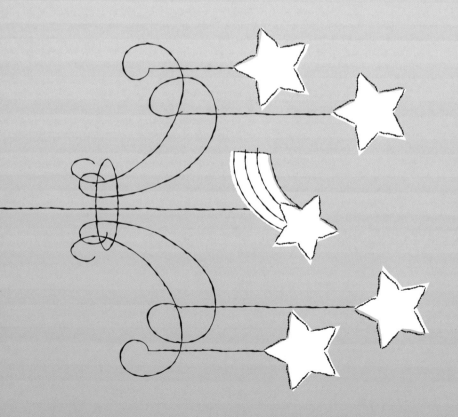

But some day, if you're lucky, and you get to stick around,
You'll have a grandbaby.... And, oh! The joy that will abound!

And just because she touched it, you will save the smallest scrap,
And miss her, even while she's sitting right there in your lap.

There's so much more than words can say. I've talked some baby talk…
But now, it's up to You and Yours to walk the baby walk.

May all your days with Baby be as full as they can be...
Don't say I didn't warn you. Hey – I wish that it was me.

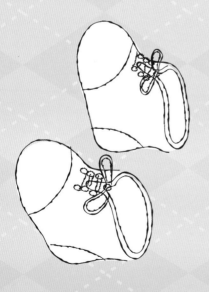

Author's Bio

Tom Hegg is a husband, father, grandfather, teacher, actor and writer. He has touched countless lives with his New York Times Best Selling title, A Cup of Christmas Tea and his series of books about "PEEF The Christmas Bear." Tom trained at Carnegie-Mellon University and won a Bush Fellowship for Graduate Study at the University of Minnesota. Tom then enjoyed several seasons with the Guthrie Theater Acting Company. He is now the Director of Drama at Breck School in Minneapolis where he holds the rank of Master Teacher. The Heggs - Tom and Peggy - are Minnesota Scandinavians who know all the jokes. Their son, Adam, and his wife, Breanne, have twice made them grandparents. Imogen Beatrice and Helena Blythe are the light of their lives.